50 Hidden Ramen Treasures Recipes

By: Kelly Johnson

Table of Contents

- Tori Paitan Ramen (Creamy Chicken Broth Ramen)
- Niboshi Ramen (Dried Sardine Broth Ramen)
- Gyokai Tonkotsu Ramen (Fish and Pork Broth Ramen)
- Hakata Black Ramen (Garlic Oil Tonkotsu Ramen)
- Wakayama Ramen (Soy Sauce and Pork Broth Ramen)
- Kurume Ramen (Original Tonkotsu Ramen)
- Tokushima Ramen (Rich Soy-Pork Broth with Egg)
- Kyoto Kotteri Ramen (Thick Chicken and Pork Ramen)
- Asahikawa Ramen (Soy Sauce Blended with Lard)
- Takayama Ramen (Clear Soy Sauce Chicken Broth)
- Katsuura Tantanmen (Spicy Soy Sauce Broth Ramen)
- Sano Ramen (Hand-Pulled Noodles with Light Broth)
- Yamagata Ramen (Chilled Soy-Based Ramen)
- Kitakata Ramen (Soy Sauce Broth with Fatty Pork)
- Onomichi Ramen (Soy Broth with Pork Back Fat)
- Kumamoto Ramen (Tonkotsu with Fried Garlic Chips)
- Muroran Curry Ramen (Hokkaido Curry-Flavored Ramen)
- Kuro Shoyu Ramen (Dark Soy Sauce Ramen from Toyama)
- Shio Butter Corn Ramen (Hokkaido Salt Ramen with Corn)
- Aomori Garlic Miso Ramen (Strong Miso Garlic Flavor)
- Kagoshima Ramen (Pork and Chicken Hybrid Broth)
- Hida Ramen (Rustic Mountain-Style Ramen)
- Sapporo Miso Ramen (Rich Miso Broth with Butter)
- Hiroshima Tsukemen (Spicy Dipping Ramen)
- Yokohama Iekei Ramen (Thick Tonkotsu-Shoyu Ramen)
- Biei Cheese Ramen (Hokkaido Cheese-Topped Ramen)
- Miyazaki Spicy Ramen (Red Chili and Chicken Broth)
- Matsumoto Soba Ramen (Buckwheat-Based Noodles in Ramen Broth)
- Aizu Black Ramen (Strong Soy Sauce Broth)
- Hakodate Shio Ramen (Clear Salt Broth)
- Katsuobushi Ramen (Dried Bonito-Flavored Ramen)
- Charred Miso Ramen (Smoky Miso-Flavored Broth)
- Ise Udon Ramen Hybrid (Thick Udon-Style Noodles in Ramen Broth)
- Senkyo Ramen (Deep Seafood and Pork Broth)
- Shimonoseki Fugu Ramen (Blowfish Broth Ramen)

- Kanazawa Curry Ramen (Curry-Flavored Broth with Pork)
- Amakusa Tori Soba (Chicken-Based Soy Sauce Ramen)
- Nishiyama Chilled Ramen (Cold Soy-Based Ramen with Ice)
- Satsuma Yuzu Ramen (Citrus-Flavored Shio Ramen)
- Kurobuta Ramen (Black Pork Ramen from Kagoshima)
- Narita Nori Ramen (Seaweed-Infused Ramen)
- Sansho Pepper Ramen (Japanese Pepper-Spiced Broth)
- Yuba Ramen (Tofu Skin-Topped Ramen)
- Echigo Sake Ramen (Broth with Fermented Sake Notes)
- Nikumiso Ramen (Ground Pork and Miso Ramen)
- Kaeshi Ramen (Traditional Soy Sauce-Base Broth)
- Kinka Saba Ramen (Golden Mackerel Broth Ramen)
- Hamanako Eel Ramen (Freshwater Eel-Based Ramen)
- Tomato Ramen (Tomato-Infused Broth with Basil)
- Sansai Ramen (Mountain Vegetable Ramen)

Tori Paitan Ramen (Creamy Chicken Broth Ramen)

Ingredients

- 2 chicken carcasses or 4 chicken thighs
- 6 cups water
- 1 onion, chopped
- 2 cloves garlic, minced
- 1-inch ginger, sliced
- 2 tbsp soy sauce
- 200g ramen noodles
- Green onions, sliced (for garnish)

Instructions

1. Simmer chicken, onion, garlic, and ginger in water for 4 hours until broth turns milky.
2. Strain broth and season with soy sauce.
3. Cook ramen noodles according to package instructions.
4. Serve noodles in broth, garnished with green onions.

Niboshi Ramen (Dried Sardine Broth Ramen)

Ingredients

- 1/2 cup dried sardines (niboshi), heads and guts removed
- 4 cups water
- 2 tbsp soy sauce
- 1 tbsp miso paste
- 200g ramen noodles
- 1 boiled egg (for garnish)

Instructions

1. Simmer niboshi in water for 1 hour, then strain.
2. Stir in soy sauce and miso paste.
3. Cook ramen noodles and serve in broth.
4. Top with a boiled egg.

Gyokai Tonkotsu Ramen (Fish and Pork Broth Ramen)

Ingredients

- 1 pork bone, cleaned
- 1/2 cup dried bonito flakes
- 6 cups water
- 1 tbsp soy sauce
- 200g ramen noodles
- Sliced pork (for topping)

Instructions

1. Simmer pork bone in water for 6 hours until rich and milky.
2. Add bonito flakes and steep for 10 minutes, then strain.
3. Season with soy sauce and serve over cooked ramen noodles.
4. Top with sliced pork.

Hakata Black Ramen (Garlic Oil Tonkotsu Ramen)

Ingredients

- 1 pork bone, cleaned
- 6 cups water
- 4 cloves garlic, minced
- 2 tbsp soy sauce
- 1 tbsp black garlic oil
- 200g thin ramen noodles

Instructions

1. Simmer pork bone in water for 6 hours until broth is milky.
2. Heat garlic in oil until blackened, then strain.
3. Cook ramen noodles and serve in broth.
4. Drizzle with black garlic oil before serving.

Wakayama Ramen (Soy Sauce and Pork Broth Ramen)

Ingredients

- 1 pork bone, cleaned
- 4 cups water
- 2 tbsp soy sauce
- 1 tbsp sake
- 200g ramen noodles
- Sliced chashu (for topping)

Instructions

1. Simmer pork bone in water for 6 hours.
2. Stir in soy sauce and sake.
3. Serve cooked ramen noodles in broth, topped with chashu.

Kurume Ramen (Original Tonkotsu Ramen)

Ingredients

- 2 pork bones, cleaned
- 6 cups water
- 1 tbsp soy sauce
- 1 tsp salt
- 200g ramen noodles
- Sliced pork belly (for topping)

Instructions

1. Simmer pork bones in water for 10 hours until broth turns thick and milky.
2. Season with soy sauce and salt.
3. Serve with cooked ramen noodles and pork belly.

Tokushima Ramen (Rich Soy-Pork Broth with Egg)

Ingredients

- 1 pork bone, cleaned
- 4 cups water
- 2 tbsp soy sauce
- 1 tbsp mirin
- 1 raw egg (for topping)
- 200g ramen noodles

Instructions

1. Simmer pork bone in water for 6 hours.
2. Stir in soy sauce and mirin.
3. Serve with cooked ramen noodles and a raw egg cracked on top.

Kyoto Kotteri Ramen (Thick Chicken and Pork Ramen)

Ingredients

- 1 chicken carcass
- 1 pork bone, cleaned
- 6 cups water
- 1 tbsp soy sauce
- 1 tbsp miso paste
- 200g ramen noodles

Instructions

1. Simmer chicken and pork bone in water for 6 hours.
2. Stir in soy sauce and miso paste.
3. Serve over cooked ramen noodles.

Asahikawa Ramen (Soy Sauce Blended with Lard)

Ingredients

- 1 pork bone, cleaned
- 4 cups water
- 2 tbsp soy sauce
- 1 tbsp lard
- 200g ramen noodles

Instructions

1. Simmer pork bone in water for 6 hours.
2. Stir in soy sauce and lard.
3. Serve over cooked ramen noodles.

Takayama Ramen (Clear Soy Sauce Chicken Broth)

Ingredients

- 1 chicken carcass
- 4 cups water
- 2 tbsp soy sauce
- 1 tbsp mirin
- 200g ramen noodles

Instructions

1. Simmer chicken carcass in water for 4 hours.
2. Stir in soy sauce and mirin.
3. Serve with cooked ramen noodles.

Katsuura Tantanmen (Spicy Soy Sauce Broth Ramen)

Ingredients

- 2 cups chicken broth
- 2 tbsp soy sauce
- 1 tbsp chili oil
- 100g ground pork
- 1/2 onion, finely chopped
- 1 clove garlic, minced
- 1 tsp sesame oil
- 200g ramen noodles
- Green onions, chopped (for garnish)

Instructions

1. Heat sesame oil in a pan and sauté garlic, onion, and ground pork.
2. Add soy sauce, chicken broth, and chili oil, then simmer.
3. Cook ramen noodles and serve in the broth.
4. Garnish with green onions.

Sano Ramen (Hand-Pulled Noodles with Light Broth)

Ingredients

- 4 cups chicken broth
- 1 tbsp soy sauce
- 1/2 tsp salt
- 200g fresh ramen noodles (or hand-pulled noodles)
- 1 slice chashu pork (for topping)
- 1/4 cup bamboo shoots

Instructions

1. Simmer chicken broth with soy sauce and salt.
2. Cook fresh ramen noodles and serve in the broth.
3. Top with chashu and bamboo shoots.

Yamagata Ramen (Chilled Soy-Based Ramen)

Ingredients

- 2 cups dashi broth
- 1 tbsp soy sauce
- 1 tsp mirin
- 1/2 tsp sugar
- 200g ramen noodles
- 1 boiled egg, halved
- 1/4 cup shredded nori

Instructions

1. Mix dashi, soy sauce, mirin, and sugar, then chill.
2. Cook ramen noodles and rinse under cold water.
3. Serve with chilled broth and top with a boiled egg and nori.

Kitakata Ramen (Soy Sauce Broth with Fatty Pork)

Ingredients

- 4 cups pork broth
- 2 tbsp soy sauce
- 1 tsp mirin
- 200g thick ramen noodles
- 2 slices fatty chashu pork

Instructions

1. Simmer pork broth with soy sauce and mirin.
2. Cook ramen noodles and serve in the broth.
3. Top with chashu pork.

Onomichi Ramen (Soy Broth with Pork Back Fat)

Ingredients

- 4 cups chicken broth
- 2 tbsp soy sauce
- 1 tbsp pork back fat, minced
- 200g ramen noodles
- 1 slice chashu pork

Instructions

1. Simmer chicken broth with soy sauce and pork back fat.
2. Cook ramen noodles and serve in the broth.
3. Top with chashu pork.

Kumamoto Ramen (Tonkotsu with Fried Garlic Chips)

Ingredients

- 4 cups pork bone broth
- 1 tbsp soy sauce
- 1 tbsp fried garlic chips
- 200g thin ramen noodles
- 1 slice chashu pork

Instructions

1. Simmer pork bone broth with soy sauce.
2. Cook ramen noodles and serve in the broth.
3. Top with garlic chips and chashu pork.

Muroran Curry Ramen (Hokkaido Curry-Flavored Ramen)

Ingredients

- 3 cups chicken broth
- 2 tbsp curry powder
- 1 tbsp soy sauce
- 1 tbsp miso paste
- 200g ramen noodles
- 1 boiled egg

Instructions

1. Simmer chicken broth with curry powder, soy sauce, and miso paste.
2. Cook ramen noodles and serve in the broth.
3. Top with a boiled egg.

Kuro Shoyu Ramen (Dark Soy Sauce Ramen from Toyama)

Ingredients

- 3 cups chicken broth
- 2 tbsp dark soy sauce
- 1 tsp mirin
- 200g ramen noodles
- 1 slice chashu pork

Instructions

1. Simmer chicken broth with dark soy sauce and mirin.
2. Cook ramen noodles and serve in the broth.
3. Top with chashu pork.

Shio Butter Corn Ramen (Hokkaido Salt Ramen with Corn)

Ingredients

- 3 cups chicken broth
- 1 tbsp salt
- 2 tbsp butter
- 1/2 cup corn kernels
- 200g ramen noodles

Instructions

1. Simmer chicken broth with salt.
2. Cook ramen noodles and serve in the broth.
3. Top with butter and corn.

Aomori Garlic Miso Ramen (Strong Miso Garlic Flavor)

Ingredients

- 3 cups pork broth
- 1 tbsp miso paste
- 2 cloves garlic, minced
- 1 tbsp soy sauce
- 200g ramen noodles

Instructions

1. Simmer pork broth with miso, soy sauce, and garlic.
2. Cook ramen noodles and serve in the broth.
3. Top with additional garlic for extra flavor.

Kagoshima Ramen (Pork and Chicken Hybrid Broth)

Ingredients

- 4 cups pork and chicken broth (made by simmering pork bones and chicken carcass for 6 hours)
- 1 tbsp soy sauce
- 1 tbsp miso paste
- 200g thick ramen noodles
- 1 slice chashu pork
- Green onions, chopped (for garnish)

Instructions

1. Simmer pork and chicken broth with soy sauce and miso paste.
2. Cook ramen noodles and serve in the broth.
3. Top with chashu and green onions.

Hida Ramen (Rustic Mountain-Style Ramen)

Ingredients

- 3 cups dashi broth
- 1 tbsp soy sauce
- 1/2 tsp salt
- 200g thin ramen noodles
- 1/4 cup mountain vegetables (shiitake, bamboo shoots)

Instructions

1. Simmer dashi broth with soy sauce and salt.
2. Cook ramen noodles and serve in the broth.
3. Top with mountain vegetables.

Sapporo Miso Ramen (Rich Miso Broth with Butter)

Ingredients

- 3 cups chicken broth
- 2 tbsp miso paste
- 1 tbsp soy sauce
- 1 tbsp butter
- 1/2 cup corn kernels
- 200g ramen noodles

Instructions

1. Simmer chicken broth with miso paste and soy sauce.
2. Cook ramen noodles and serve in the broth.
3. Top with butter and corn.

Hiroshima Tsukemen (Spicy Dipping Ramen)

Ingredients

- 3 cups dashi broth
- 2 tbsp soy sauce
- 1 tbsp chili oil
- 200g ramen noodles (served cold)
- 1 boiled egg, halved

Instructions

1. Mix dashi broth, soy sauce, and chili oil, then chill.
2. Cook ramen noodles, rinse under cold water, and drain.
3. Serve noodles with dipping sauce and boiled egg.

Yokohama Iekei Ramen (Thick Tonkotsu-Shoyu Ramen)

Ingredients

- 4 cups pork bone broth
- 1 tbsp soy sauce
- 200g thick ramen noodles
- 1 boiled egg
- 1 sheet nori (seaweed)

Instructions

1. Simmer pork bone broth with soy sauce.
2. Cook ramen noodles and serve in the broth.
3. Top with boiled egg and nori.

Biei Cheese Ramen (Hokkaido Cheese-Topped Ramen)

Ingredients

- 3 cups chicken broth
- 1 tbsp miso paste
- 1/2 cup shredded Hokkaido cheese
- 200g ramen noodles

Instructions

1. Simmer chicken broth with miso paste.
2. Cook ramen noodles and serve in the broth.
3. Top with shredded cheese and let it melt.

Miyazaki Spicy Ramen (Red Chili and Chicken Broth)

Ingredients

- 3 cups chicken broth
- 1 tbsp miso paste
- 1 tsp chili flakes
- 200g ramen noodles

Instructions

1. Simmer chicken broth with miso paste and chili flakes.
2. Cook ramen noodles and serve in the broth.

Matsumoto Soba Ramen (Buckwheat-Based Noodles in Ramen Broth)

Ingredients

- 3 cups soy-based ramen broth
- 200g soba noodles
- 1 tbsp mirin
- 1 boiled egg

Instructions

1. Simmer ramen broth with mirin.
2. Cook soba noodles and serve in the broth.
3. Top with a boiled egg.

Aizu Black Ramen (Strong Soy Sauce Broth)

Ingredients

- 3 cups chicken broth
- 3 tbsp dark soy sauce
- 200g ramen noodles
- 1 slice chashu pork

Instructions

1. Simmer chicken broth with dark soy sauce.
2. Cook ramen noodles and serve in the broth.
3. Top with chashu pork.

Hakodate Shio Ramen (Clear Salt Broth)

Ingredients

- 4 cups chicken broth
- 1 tbsp salt
- 1 tsp soy sauce
- 200g thin ramen noodles
- 1 slice chashu pork
- 1 boiled egg, halved
- Green onions, sliced

Instructions

1. Simmer chicken broth with salt and soy sauce.
2. Cook ramen noodles and serve in the broth.
3. Top with chashu, boiled egg, and green onions.

Katsuobushi Ramen (Dried Bonito-Flavored Ramen)

Ingredients

- 4 cups dashi broth (made with dried bonito flakes)
- 1 tbsp soy sauce
- 1 tbsp mirin
- 200g ramen noodles
- 1/4 cup bonito flakes (for topping)

Instructions

1. Simmer dashi broth with soy sauce and mirin.
2. Cook ramen noodles and serve in the broth.
3. Top with additional bonito flakes.

Charred Miso Ramen (Smoky Miso-Flavored Broth)

Ingredients

- 3 cups chicken broth
- 2 tbsp miso paste
- 1/2 onion, charred
- 1 clove garlic, charred
- 200g ramen noodles

Instructions

1. Char the onion and garlic over an open flame or in a hot pan.
2. Simmer broth with miso paste, onion, and garlic.
3. Cook ramen noodles and serve in the broth.

Ise Udon Ramen Hybrid (Thick Udon-Style Noodles in Ramen Broth)

Ingredients

- 4 cups pork-based ramen broth
- 200g thick udon-style ramen noodles
- 1 tbsp soy sauce
- 1 boiled egg, halved

Instructions

1. Simmer pork-based broth with soy sauce.
2. Cook thick ramen noodles and serve in the broth.
3. Top with a boiled egg.

Senkyo Ramen (Deep Seafood and Pork Broth)

Ingredients

- 3 cups pork broth
- 1 cup seafood broth (made from shrimp shells and dried fish)
- 1 tbsp soy sauce
- 200g ramen noodles
- 1 shrimp, grilled (for topping)

Instructions

1. Simmer pork and seafood broth together with soy sauce.
2. Cook ramen noodles and serve in the broth.
3. Top with grilled shrimp.

Shimonoseki Fugu Ramen (Blowfish Broth Ramen)

Ingredients

- 4 cups blowfish broth (made by simmering fugu bones)
- 1 tbsp sake
- 1 tsp salt
- 200g thin ramen noodles

Instructions

1. Simmer blowfish broth with sake and salt.
2. Cook ramen noodles and serve in the broth.

Kanazawa Curry Ramen (Curry-Flavored Broth with Pork)

Ingredients

- 3 cups chicken broth
- 2 tbsp Japanese curry roux
- 1 tbsp soy sauce
- 200g ramen noodles
- 1 slice pork cutlet (for topping)

Instructions

1. Simmer chicken broth with curry roux and soy sauce.
2. Cook ramen noodles and serve in the broth.
3. Top with a pork cutlet.

Amakusa Tori Soba (Chicken-Based Soy Sauce Ramen)

Ingredients

- 4 cups chicken broth
- 1 tbsp soy sauce
- 200g thin ramen noodles
- 1 grilled chicken thigh (for topping)

Instructions

1. Simmer chicken broth with soy sauce.
2. Cook ramen noodles and serve in the broth.
3. Top with grilled chicken thigh.

Nishiyama Chilled Ramen (Cold Soy-Based Ramen with Ice)

Ingredients

- 3 cups dashi broth
- 1 tbsp soy sauce
- 1 tsp sugar
- 200g ramen noodles
- Ice cubes

Instructions

1. Chill dashi broth and mix with soy sauce and sugar.
2. Cook ramen noodles, rinse under cold water, and drain.
3. Serve with ice cubes in the broth.

Satsuma Yuzu Ramen (Citrus-Flavored Shio Ramen)

Ingredients

- 4 cups chicken broth
- 1 tbsp salt
- 1 tbsp yuzu juice
- 1 tsp soy sauce
- 200g thin ramen noodles
- 1 slice chashu pork
- 1 tsp yuzu zest (for garnish)
- Green onions, chopped

Instructions

1. Simmer chicken broth with salt, soy sauce, and yuzu juice.
2. Cook ramen noodles and serve in the broth.
3. Top with chashu pork, yuzu zest, and green onions.

Kurobuta Ramen (Black Pork Ramen from Kagoshima)

Ingredients

- 4 cups pork bone broth
- 1 tbsp soy sauce
- 200g thick ramen noodles
- 2 slices kurobuta pork belly (slow-cooked)
- 1 boiled egg, halved
- 1/4 cup bamboo shoots

Instructions

1. Simmer pork bone broth with soy sauce.
2. Cook ramen noodles and serve in the broth.
3. Top with kurobuta pork, boiled egg, and bamboo shoots.

Narita Nori Ramen (Seaweed-Infused Ramen)

Ingredients

- 4 cups dashi broth
- 2 tbsp soy sauce
- 1/2 sheet nori, shredded (plus extra for garnish)
- 200g ramen noodles
- 1 boiled egg, halved

Instructions

1. Simmer dashi broth with soy sauce and shredded nori.
2. Cook ramen noodles and serve in the broth.
3. Top with additional nori and a boiled egg.

Sansho Pepper Ramen (Japanese Pepper-Spiced Broth)

Ingredients

- 3 cups chicken broth
- 1 tbsp miso paste
- 1 tsp soy sauce
- 1/2 tsp ground sansho pepper
- 200g ramen noodles
- Green onions, chopped

Instructions

1. Simmer chicken broth with miso paste, soy sauce, and sansho pepper.
2. Cook ramen noodles and serve in the broth.
3. Garnish with green onions.

Yuba Ramen (Tofu Skin-Topped Ramen)

Ingredients

- 4 cups soy milk-based broth
- 1 tbsp miso paste
- 1 tsp soy sauce
- 200g ramen noodles
- 1/4 cup yuba (tofu skin), torn into strips

Instructions

1. Simmer soy milk broth with miso paste and soy sauce.
2. Cook ramen noodles and serve in the broth.
3. Top with yuba strips before serving.

Echigo Sake Ramen (Broth with Fermented Sake Notes)

Ingredients

- 3 cups chicken broth
- 1/4 cup sake
- 1 tbsp soy sauce
- 1 tsp mirin
- 200g ramen noodles
- 1 slice chashu pork
- Green onions, chopped (for garnish)

Instructions

1. Simmer chicken broth with sake, soy sauce, and mirin.
2. Cook ramen noodles and serve in the broth.
3. Top with chashu and green onions.

Nikumiso Ramen (Ground Pork and Miso Ramen)

Ingredients

- 3 cups pork broth
- 2 tbsp miso paste
- 1 tbsp soy sauce
- 100g ground pork
- 1 clove garlic, minced
- 200g ramen noodles
- Green onions, chopped

Instructions

1. Sauté ground pork and garlic until browned.
2. Add pork broth, miso paste, and soy sauce, then simmer.
3. Cook ramen noodles and serve in the broth.
4. Top with green onions and ground pork.

Kaeshi Ramen (Traditional Soy Sauce-Base Broth)

Ingredients

- 4 cups dashi broth
- 2 tbsp soy sauce
- 1 tbsp mirin
- 1 tsp sugar
- 200g ramen noodles
- 1 slice chashu pork

Instructions

1. Simmer dashi broth with soy sauce, mirin, and sugar.
2. Cook ramen noodles and serve in the broth.
3. Top with chashu pork.

Kinka Saba Ramen (Golden Mackerel Broth Ramen)

Ingredients

- 3 cups mackerel-based fish broth
- 1 tbsp soy sauce
- 1 tsp miso paste
- 200g ramen noodles
- 1 grilled mackerel fillet (for topping)

Instructions

1. Simmer fish broth with soy sauce and miso paste.
2. Cook ramen noodles and serve in the broth.
3. Top with grilled mackerel.

Hamanako Eel Ramen (Freshwater Eel-Based Ramen)

Ingredients

- 3 cups eel-based broth (made from simmering eel bones)
- 1 tbsp soy sauce
- 200g ramen noodles
- 1 grilled eel fillet, sliced

Instructions

1. Simmer eel broth with soy sauce.
2. Cook ramen noodles and serve in the broth.
3. Top with grilled eel slices.

Tomato Ramen (Tomato-Infused Broth with Basil)

Ingredients

- 3 cups chicken broth
- 1/2 cup pureed tomatoes
- 1 tbsp soy sauce
- 1 tsp sugar
- 200g ramen noodles
- Fresh basil leaves

Instructions

1. Simmer chicken broth with tomato puree, soy sauce, and sugar.
2. Cook ramen noodles and serve in the broth.
3. Garnish with fresh basil leaves.

Sansai Ramen (Mountain Vegetable Ramen)

Ingredients

- 3 cups dashi broth
- 1 tbsp soy sauce
- 1/2 cup mixed mountain vegetables (shiitake, bamboo shoots, fern shoots)
- 200g ramen noodles

Instructions

1. Simmer dashi broth with soy sauce.
2. Add mountain vegetables and cook for 3 minutes.
3. Serve over ramen noodles.

www.ingramcontent.com/pod-product-compliance
Lightning Source LLC
LaVergne TN
LVHW081339060526
838201LV00055B/2735